I, ODYSSEUS

I, ODYSSEUS

poems

by

LEO AYLEN

SIDGWICK & JACKSON
LONDON

©1971 by Leo Aylen

ISBN 0.283.48480.2

Printed in Great Britain by
Specialised Offset Services, Liverpool
and Wood, Westworth & Co. Ltd., St. Helens
for Sidgwick and Jackson Limited
1 Tavistock Chambers, Bloomsbury Way
London, W.C.1.

For Annette

Contents

I, Odysseus . . . 10

Love charm . . . 19

The departure of the gods . . . 20

Dissolving images

        Sestina . . . 22

        Percival . . . 24

El Dorado . . . 25

The birth of Aeneas . . . 26

'Do take a seat' . . . 28

Epphatha . . . 30

'And for all this, nature is never spent,' . . . 31

'Let there be light' . . . 34

. . . A white Christ . . . 35

For an unborn child . . . 37

Birth of Aphrodite . . . 38

Cucumber girl . . . 39

The pearl-plunge . . . 40

Full-fed . . . 41

Green moon . . . 42

The doom-breakers . . . 42

Manstain . . . 43

The bee's song to the dead-nettle . . . 44

Shula . . . 44

Carbon-monoxide . . . 45

Gargoyle . . . 46

Translations from the Greek . . . 47

    The Hoopoe's Aubade . . . 48

    The Hoopoe's Invocation of the Birds . . . 48

    The Nightingale Song . . . 49

    from the Parabasis of 'The Birds' . . . 50

The meeting of Odysseus and Penelope . . . 51

Orestes' urn . . . 56

The death of Oedipus . . . 58

NOTE

The poems which are illustrated are reproduced from the author's own handwriting.

I, Odysseus

Note. In the Odyssey, book 10, the companions of Odysseus are turned into pigs by the magic of Circe the witch goddess, but Odysseus himself escapes through the counter-charm of the root moly, given him by Hermes, the winged messenger god, who escorts the souls to death. In the Odyssey book 12, Odysseus has to sail past the Sirens whose utterly beautiful song lures all men who hear it on to the rocks of their island to die. On the advice of Circe, Odysseus blocks his men's ears with beeswax, so that they can't hear the song, while he makes them strap him to the mast so that he can hear the song, but cannot of course free himself to land.

In the Purgatorio, Canto 19, Dante dreams of a Siren, but Virgil and Lady Reason between them quickly dispose of her as his evil fantasy.

I have added to the myth by making Circe a sister of the Sirens, and made use of the equivalence of Hermes to the Roman god, Mercury, and so the metal mercury or quicksilver.

Mavrodaphne is a Cretan wine, dark sweet and heavy, quite unlike the normal resinated Greek wine.

(i) Prelude

              .... I seem to see them
As time gaped open ...
                I seem to will them
Recumbent into flesh, by the blank Aegaean.
Milky Circe, and the Sirens her sisters,
Giggling the tunes of their murderous spells.

"Honey and darkness mavrodaphne cushions,
Embrace the guzzle of earth,
Nuzzle the kissing roots," whispers Circe.

"Scud in the wind like grit over tide-line
Silver ripple of misty sand-spray
Breath of dust forever in motion"
Sing the pale Sirens like dive of gannets.

"Charming your grit" sweetly laughs Circe.
"My wine-honey roots enmesh men into four-legged snufflers."
Her dark simper, milky with poison.

"Our desire is a man whose savour remains
Bitter droplet in sweetest wine-bowl.
Only such bones are fit for the waves to bleach.
Only such grit is worthy of grinding to pearl."

The simpering sisters parted for ever
To finger their islands sensual for human extinction
As my wing-god appeared,
His palm cupped round the dark twisted root of moonlight,
Goblet with quicksilver droplet of bitterness,
Resinous droplet of bitterness
Cupped in his palm like the scent of a wine,
Like a soul to escort beyond death . . . .

(ii) Circe's Night

Dark water tonguing the moon-silver sand-sparkle,
Dark mavrodaphne, sleep soothing
My drunk shipmates like brayed jewels,
Sweet wine lady I enter your cushions
Mix with your foam of dark honey
Relish your fullness
Dark tongue lapping the sparkle.
Now mavrodaphne, the secret.
And all, all, all . . . .

"No" she teased,
Tickling my nose with her featherlike finger,
"Rest like your shipmates, you who are whole,
You who are jewel not to be pounded,
Not to be swamped by the foaming darkness
Or melted like wax in the honey sun,
Rest content with your mastery.
Learn no more.
Enter.
Relish my darkness."

Enter I will.
Relish I will.
Taste you and take your secret.
So come, mavrodaphne, don't mock me,
The twisted root who crawls through your pool of moonlight.
Us, we are not to be blended.
Only to meet, embrace,
Exchange our secrets and part.
So come mavrodaphne
Mock me no longer.
The secret. Yield.

"Darkness there is where a man must rest and enquire no further.
And darkness where men clench fist on their moly,
This is the silver secret," she said.
"Silver as bleaching bones
Ground by the wind to a shimmering ripple
Of white sand stung by the spray-singing oyster ladies
Irridescent cascading mothers of pearl
Endlessly tonguing the homeless flesh of sailors.
There's the secret, my resin lover,
I'll exchange for the foam of your grappling hands."

Yes, and in you tonight my hands will be foaming gladly.
But these irridescent cascades
Over salt-scarred flesh
And sea-ground bones
These tongues are old friends from childhood.
I thought in a ripping of panic you'd opened the sweetness,
The sweet abscess,
Exposing your demons sliding and writhing inside.
But such a salt spray taste is easy.

"Oh no" she said,
And the dark heaved laughter like waves over shipwreck.
"That was the rind of my secret.
The writhing heart you've already eaten,
Swallowed, digested, absorbed,
That root from Hermes.
Now, now,
You who knew only the bleaching wind
Will see the wind singers and be clamped to their language
Till you're hammered translucent like grit to a pearl
As the rock screams . . .
Screams . . .
Screams . . ."

Then the shivering crunched into action.

Resin's oozed into your wine, mavrodaphne.
Oh lap me close.
Defend me, dissolve me,
Soften my acid heart in your honey-foam sparkling darkness
For one night only,
For now.
For now. . .

"What and charm you to pig-man" she giggled.
"You who chose bitterness,
Who chose root undissolving in darkness,
Grit that's turning to pearl inside me,
Twisted root crawling in mastery over my honeyed moonlight,
Oh yes, you'll take my secret,
And pay,
And pay
My stinging demons
All, all, all . . .
But now . . . "

Shuddering gathered and pounded inside me,
But hive-melting honey flooded in spasms,
And the bees sang . . .

"Take wax" she said later,
"My home of sweetness to knead in your hands,
With the sun to help you, my winged lover,
Kneading and pugging the honey home
Into a sweet, soft, gummy ear-clogger
To stuff, block and deafen your peasants,
Your melted comrades,
From feeling the spray sting of the oyster ladies
And being the grit that's spurned by a mother of pearl,
While you who came chewing that bitterness root from the wing-god,
Face and embrace my demons,
Strap yourself to the resin of your pine-mast,
Chew your moly
That mocked and mastered my spell of dark honey
And melted me in this embrace of velvet.
Chew your bitterness . . .
Oh but honey-melter, wing-spreading, pine-mast lover,
Soon to be bleached into silver and incense,
I give you, clutched with your moly,
My home of sweetness to knead in your hands . . .
Now, now, now . . . "

Then shuddering bounded inside me, a shipwreck
Of clattering sinews, a spasm
Thudding with sweat till I tasted an ocean
Whose darkness foamed. . . .

(iii) Sirens

    AIH. SSSSSSS.
    Stop. Cut the ropes.
    Pig-men I'm changing my orders.
    Untie me.
    How could I let you
    Lash me to a mast with boatswain's lanyards,
    I who was splashing the wine-lady's goblet
    And foaming into her cushions
    While you're snuffling through your mates' shit for acorns.
    Pig-men.
    Your ears blocked with bee mastication.
    AIH. SSSSSSS.
    Cut the ropes.
    We've reached the secret,
    The silver and incense,
    The killer pearl.
    Cut the ropes you snuffling deaf-mutes.
    This is the secret,
    The trap
    That snaps shut on all honey-dark islands.
    This wine's the resin of pine-mast fit for a longship
    Fit to sail through the pillars of Heracles
    Fit to sail into the split of the lightning
    Welding the thunderclaps into an island,
    A cloudy Symplegades, to volplane past laughing,
    Fit to sail up Hell's river of blood,
    Splash through the shallows of Lethe
    And land on the absent-minded shore of Elysium.
    This is the secret, this is the trap.
    Space blind white light singing
    Now let me die . . .
    Oh this is your secret my lady Circe,
    Grit scarred into my soul till a world full of pig men
    Deign to tear out my ears.
    This is the secret, this is the trap.
    This is the trap, the grit and the pearl.
    Wings, wings, wings . . .
    AIH. SSSSSSS.

(iv) Mount Purgatory

Now I'm grown-up they tell me the whole thing's a dream,
Dream of lame woman, squinting, stunted,
Club-footed, stuttering. I'm the sun.
I'm the sun, so they say, the Aegaean sunshine
That melts this wax-work into a Siren,
Kissing my own spit into a jewel,
Tonguing my own wide oceans into a pearl.

Oh Circe, on your forgotten island . . . .

Virgil and Lady Reason between them
Pulled up this Siren's skirt and shewed me her varicose veins.
"This is your trap" they said, "this is your secret.
This is your blind white beauty — a drab,
Squeezed like foul-smelling ointment out of your dreams."
They laughed to think that anyone might be frightened,
As they poured out cups of non-alcoholic syrup.

Oh Circe, on your forgotten island . . .

One night of foaming vintage . . .
You whose limp arms and velvet banquet
Charm in sweet moments of darkness all, all Virgilian philosophers
With a flip of the wand to shit-snuffling porkers,
Smiling across at your sisters the Sirens,
Sweeter and softer and older and darker than Reason you saw
    your revenge
On me and those sisters of yours together:
Me your lover, your only lover,
Your only man with resin of mastery
Droplet of bitterness still reflection

Remaining clear in your rippling goblet
Of embracing, softening, poisoning mavrodaphne,
Me, tied to the sting of their spell,
Blown for ever on silver dust-waves,
But conscious for ever to mock them,
Never allowed the sleep to which dust is entitled,
The sleep that I chose in your arms to discard for this wind
    that's ripping my ears,
And I, who lying with you once craved to be melted,
To lose my bitter savour, my root in Hermes,
Who, tied to the mast, screamed at the silver torture,
The pounding to pearl.
Who longed to succumb to the sleep of the bleaching bones,
Now, older and wiser, with reasonable voices round me,
Yet choose to be what I am,
Your lover of one night only,
Tied to the pearl itself, the royal torture,
Bitterness sweeter than sun-blackened honey
Drenched with resin from woods of Elysium,
Ooze from a pine-mast kindled as incense
By the fondling song of cliff-splitting bone-polishing ocean.

Let Sirens grind me,
Lady Reason cluck "Nothing's the matter"
I choose to be pearl,
That droplet you saw, bitter and clear, in your own dark winebowl,
A quicksilver pearl, a hole in your face's reflection,
Quicksilver drop from the wing-god's own phial of bitterness,
Hermes, the wing-god, guider of souls to death.

And now, deserted, the wing-god vanished,
Clutching my hand on a twist of darkened moonlight,
No sight in my aeon-blind eyes of your wax or your cushions,
No sound in my ears of wind over sand-spray,
I grope stray phantoms past me down bottomless darkness . . .

And now, now, now . . .

In a blank for ever . . .

Help me . . .

Love Charm

Once for gold and twice for gold
And thrice for crimson blood.

Once for gold and the night of a queen
With thousands of sunflowers bursting her crown;
Sunflower kittens and shooting stars
Tambourines made of thistledown.

Once for gold and twice for gold
And thrice for crimson blood.

Twice for gold of ocean's wealth,
Sea horse wheels with opal eyes,
Goblets of reflected chrysolite
Whirring the sheen of dragonflies.

Once for gold and twice for gold
And thrice for crimson blood.

Thrice for an ever opening rose
Of thorns and blood and molten cave
Where sea-horse sunflower withers and falls
And wounds gallop into the welcoming grave.

Once for gold and twice for gold
And thrice for crimson blood.

HESELTINE

The departure of the gods

ἐρημία γὰρ πόλιν ὅταν λάβῃ κακή, νοσεῖ
τὰ των θεῶν οὐδὲ τιμᾶσθαι θέλει

When emptiness comes to a city
The gods catch the sickness.
There's no more call for worship.

       I am Poseidon, whose white horses
       Wallop on boat decks at the flip of my finger.
       I am Poseidon, and I am departing.
       Trojans, your town is in flames, so your gods desert you.
       We, whose power is association
       with law of nature to build or destroy —
       To flourish flying fish, or rip a mainsail —
       Can only appear as personal protectors
       Given an altar, a place for worship
       At regular times, for thus our power
       Is localised for good or evil.

       Trojans, the spirit has left you.
       I am a spirit.

       Why?
       Why is a word for the All-embracing Justice,
       Erasing cities with his time,
       Till homes and temples and home-loving heroes —
       This "Troy" — turns into a meaningless syllable
       As I Poseidon vanish.

       Trojans . . .

       If gods could weep, I'd flood the land with tears.

       Trojans, Trojans, . . .

What consolation is there to offer —
Except the assurance of All-embracing Justice —
Embracing you, Cassandra, with Greek rape,
Scratching its hysterical fingers, Hecuba, through your hair,
And capering with you round your blazing grandson . . .

Trojans, my Trojans . . .

But at least you will find some sort of immortality
In the fairy-tale called history.
I shall be only an item in its prop-box:
Tawdry gilt figurehead nicknamed Poseidon.
For once spirit has left the ocean
How can men conceive it except as mindless.

Mortals I envy you your weeping
Less than Hecuba's hacking laughter.
May I like her before I vanish
Cackle and split myself in pieces
So my future masters struggle to safety
Through fragments of their friends while the waves chuckle
In a last cacophony . . .
     last cackle . . .
Lassss cac . . cac . .
     lasssssss chuckllllllllle
Crack . . .

Dissolving images

Sestina

Dissolving images, halated faces,
Quicksilver girl. Starlight sprayed on my silence.
Clear eyes offered in answer to all questions,
Which shed their marble, stain their light with jewels,
Paint mouths to suck and heave, sweat, scream and open
In desperate midsummer midnight dreams.

Follow these sheep to Sarum where the dream
Of Arthur-Alfred rises. Oaks breathe, faces
Of acorn druids peer, grow, call the open
Downland to gallop, wheel, retire, with silent
Horse-hooves. Then a thousand years shrinks to the jewel
Of Athelney, and art-historians' questions.

Waterless Delos. Gone the myth. Here, question
This island. Yes. It floated, Aegaean dream
Where fountains sleep-walking gush rainbow jewelled
Rivulet lyre notes, baby Appollos, faces
Of foam-flecked Nereids — Sound lyre, sound . . sound silence.
Tourist pavilion built where his cave opened.

Heave the nail-studded door, groan hinges open,
Blinded by out of the sun, the gold, the question
Of God, the dark, the red and royal blue, dream-
thin, stained glass windows. Dark. Such dove-filled silence.
Where are those credos thundering from packed faces
Gaping for pearl of price, the answer jewel?

Ebony image, polished to a jewel
By seas of hands rolling the curtain open
On thudding drums, feet stamping, pearl-eyed faces.
Can their trance wave an answer to our questions?
Biafra's dugs are dry. Your thornbush dreams
Worn smooth as ebony wait in starved silence.

Here dolly, where pneumatic drills rape silent
My polystyrene girl's synthetic jewel
Glittering cathode ray of parlour dreams,
Here concrete towers fell, the rooms ripped open,
Drug-taking hands shook, Ginsberg posed his question.
Starved look Druid lyre liar bearded faces.

Pasty the tea-shop faces dream-gorged silence.
Questions dissect the eyes still, cutting jewels
Opening midnight caves on waterless dreams.

Percival

    Percival entered the dragon's cave
    Tensed for the shock of a belching flame;
    Then tiptoed groping along the wall,
    But for black leagues no sound came.

    He'd an apple and a rose for the dragon's slave
    Whose breath is petals, whose hair is flame red,
    Who is strapped to a rock by the central fire.
    The apple grew gritty from dust and sweat

    As he tensed with fear and clenched his hand
    Imagining sudden blasts of heat.
    But for mile after mile he heard nothing,
    Only his own slow, dust-shuffling, feet.

    He reached the place after five-hundred years.
    Nothing was left of the fire but ash
    And a bottomless hole. He dribbled a stone
    And listened, but never heard thud or splash.

    No girl was bound to the pillar of rock,
    Ages ago she'd been burnt away.
    Only a niche with a tarnished cup
    Of silver so blackened it looked like clay.

    And his rose was only a spike of thorns
    His apple was only a rotten core.
    Though thin light fell through a crack in the roof
    By now he couldn't tell light for sure.

    But he smashed the apple and scattered the pips
    In the ashes where once the fire had burned,
    And crushed the rose thorn into his hand,
    To find if he could still bleed from a wound.

    He groped in the ashes, and found no bones,
    But the cup when he tapped it gave a ring.
    He thought of a song for the slave-girl's soul,
    But died before he had started to sing.

El Dorado

Dry phlegm scraping his throat for a cry
That croaks "Those braceleted gestures lie,
There's only this vulture racketing sky
White as marriage at noon.

"Beyond the hills there's gold" they said,
"Past the gully where earth opens red
As the moistening lips of a girl in bed
White as marriage at noon.

"Beyond the hills unrolls the lake,
Ripples to fondle your salt-flayed ache" —
Words as void as this high rock flake
White as marriage at noon.

Gold in his arms looks blacker than coal
Hooves in his head like a happy black foal
Trotting into the sun that bright black hole ..
White as marriage at noon

Dry phlegm scraping his throat for a cry
To break from the vulture racketing sky;
Crackling to parchment he staggers to his
White as marriage at noon.

The birth of Aeneas

The goddess floats on the waves like foam
Shakes the surf from her frothy hair
Glides up a gully to the top of the cliff
Her nostrils quivering in the mountain air.

The lord Anchises sits watching his sheep.
The hairs on his fingers flash like gold
As he lifts his sheep whistle into the sun
And his fingers flicker to stop the holes.

Aphrodite appeared as a filmy haze
Of desire for male flesh, for a body of earth,
In the picnic mood which claims to relish
Food with that bitter taste from dirt.

She dressed herself with mortality
In order to touch his sweat-streaked cheek,
She stained herself with the juice of death
To have legs to open, and be mounted like sheep

And lie as animal in his arms
Feeling a mortal muscle's power.
On prickly grass she almost forgot
Her nature as goddess . . . for half an hour.

A bee caught wind of her nectar breath
And as she laid her cheek on his,
It came for a suck of the Flower of flowers,
And stung them both as they moved to kiss.

She twinged as she felt the ridiculous pain,
And though Anchises pulled out the sting,
She turned herself back to a goddess at once,
A film of heat-haze, vanishing . . .

The Lover-of-Laughter's son never smiled.
His Rome, his world-wide empire, began
With a pious gaze at Dido in flames
And a word of command. "Row. Hard as you can."

'Do take a seat'

"Do take a seat" they said politely.
"I'm sure
You're
Able to explain."

Mustard suit yapped at my ankles
Like a toothless chihua-hua.
Out of the fat one's voluminous navel
Crawled, smiling brightly, adders.

"I'm sure" they beamed like archbishops,
"I'm sure
You're
Able to explain."

In your mustard suit and salmon shirt
I can't abide you Mr Splurt.
As for you Mr Blockitt
I retch when I see you without your jacket.

Their beam became a Colgate grin.
"I'm sure
       I'm sure
You'll explain
           You'll explain
Ever —
    ever —
ry thing.
      ry thing.

The adders morris dancing
Round the dug down maypole of his navel.
Cows chewed pink Splurt berries
Whose heart, like yew,
Is greenish yellow, . . . poisonous.

Mouth-frothing, the cows fell dead.
"Pity" they said.
"Still," with a sigh of relief,
"We can freeze the meat for Oxfam."

Adders cuddle Blockitt's nipples
Licking the matted jungle of his armpits.
His belly flows over his waistband like the Orinoco.
"Everything" they said with a smile.
Their minds are big and broad and wide.

"Ev . . . er . . . y . . . thing.

Ever
    ever
Ry thing
      ry thing.
Thing."

"Thing" they said, and kicked me to the floor,
Fastened electrodes on to my brain,
Drained me into a small pipette
Which Mr Blockitt
Put in his pocket.
Then covered my black remains
With last week's coloured supplement
And switched on TV.

"Re
Thing"
They said.
"Now that he's . . .
Dead . . .
I think that closes the meeting."

Epphatha

Oh they told me all about the great musics,
Breathing their sighs over my apricot blossom
Tremulously as violin harmonics,
Pattering their fingers and shaking water
To show the ripples of piano and harp,
Or squatting their arse for horn and trumpet
With a smirk of in-group approval.

Oh yes, they were ever so conscientious
At telling me all about great music,
When sound for me was a consonantless tone
And weasels chewing my ears.

So now that God has spat on the weasels
It's not their trumpets,
Still less the organ's consonantless tone,
The sounds of great music, that I clutch to my ears
Like water the second day in desert,
It's the noises they never thought to mention,
Twitch of blanket,
Difference of rubbing thumb over forefinger
Thumb over ring-finger,
The consonants in itch and scratch and rustle.

Let greater, wiser, crueller, kinder than me
Praise the great symphonies.
Let my thanks sound in the ears of God
Like the cheeky scratching of grasshopper thighs
And the march of . . . woodlice.

'And for all this, nature is never spent,'
G.M. Hopkins

    Now.
    Here,
    Where the fishy-eyed men ant round in their perspex bubbles
    And the old heap in her concrete falsies
    Perfumes her fanny with squirts of liquid detergent,

    Here, even here,
    Enter the space inside.
    Push through the purple curtains
    That finger your eyelids.

    Wait.
    Wash the traffic away in a damburst of rivers.
    (Mud heaves up and hardens to granite.)
    Wait for the island.

    Girders are snapping at herds of elephant waves
    Trundling off bridges on whistling barrows of fruit.
    Hammers fall silent.
    Poundings cease.
    Fishy-eyed men pass final memos
    And die gasping bubbles of indigo gas.

    Wait.
    Rises the island
    Here.

The sugar-fed river gallops under us
Thousands of peacocks with oilstain eyes
Perched on his beige frothing mane
Sniffing and mounting our bitch of an island on heat
Who lifts her tail and dodges the froth
Of the fishy-eyed men dressed up in detergent bottles.

Oh my island
Split their speedboats on your feathers of granite
That skin my fingertips scrambling your gullies,
Splinter their brains and abide.

Here let us be
Violet
As oaks crash round us in orange storms,
Violet inviolate
In dark caves of tumbled timber
Lit by reflection of golden aconite.
Here
Wait.

The cold-eyed men whoosh out to sea like memos in bottles
Swept under carpets of plankton.
Our island abides.

Oh the elephant laughter forests have vanished,
But so have the concrete falsies.
Here
Over stripped bare oilstained granite
Desert thorns of rusty stanchions
Windowless walless spirals of disconnected tottering fire-escape
Here,
Over bare rock, volplane the sea-mews,
Herring gull, black-back, tern and kittiwake,
Here perches gob-stuffing cormorant,
Carrousels racket the air and their shit
Struts over the rock like puffins.

Back creeps heather
Cowering whortleberries
Till there, there, there,
There in a sun-sucking hollow
Peeps out the golden impudence of Heartsease.

There
Wait.

In the peeping golden space inside.

Then take the spade . . .

'Let there be light'

Let there be light.
And light jack-in-a-boxed its tail into sea-horses
Sack-racing up through clear water
To tickle the humming-birds' unicorn darting through cracks
    in the sunrise.

Larches burst into filigree waterfalls,
Quartz splits, and thousands on thousands
Of galloping silver unicorn hooves
Thunder the salt beds, kicking up myriads
Of vanishing diamonds
Halating the race track of spiders' webs . . .
O rider of unicorns, cataract down through our halls
With spadefuls, galleons of light.
Let there be bright —

But the waste-coated slug man
Smearing the earth with his well-greased
Plasticine excrement
Tortures the fish of the light till it chokes in his
    pink-stoppered bottles
Planted on every shore,
Puffing black clouds for the light to wear overcoats,
Then pumping it pure through sterilised perspex
Measured with infinitesimal exactness
(Ten milligrams light to one square inch)
Till it hardens to rigid detergent bubbles
With which slug man is replanting the earth
Beneath the warm dark clouds oozing out of his underclothes.

...A white Christ...

...and then high on the skyline with snow behind him
A white Christ
Diamond, sliding the waterfalls,
White silhouetted on white,
Tossing and bouncing in spume from the boulders
In the tiny bullets of spume that catapult skywards,
Whiteness collecting each bubble's rainbow,
A white stream for ever descending
For ever on rock points shattered,
But down, down,
Resting a moment, bridging the gulley
With each foot poised on a hovering eagle,
Then down, down, leaping and tossing,
Trampoline springs from the spit of a spume bullet,
And then down again, down like swoop of an eagle,
Down like eagle's black dot in the sun —
Black with golden aura —
But him, white, white in the sun,
White with the golden aura,
White, white, white as the streamers
Of plunging, deafening, for ever thundering foam
Shot up by the push of the feet-slashing rocks —
The snow behind pouring light down the gulley —
Swinging on streamers, creepers of foam,
Gibbon and eagle, Caesar the juggler
Collared and furred with spray,
Down with a side-step, a skip and a somersault
To grip the trapeze with his teeth in a dive
Down, down, down on the light off the snowridge
Tossing his crystals of opal and amethyst
Into this flicker of sun through young beech-leaves
This secret pool
This pale, green-golden spinel,
In which, for a moment, we lie,
And whispering...Come...

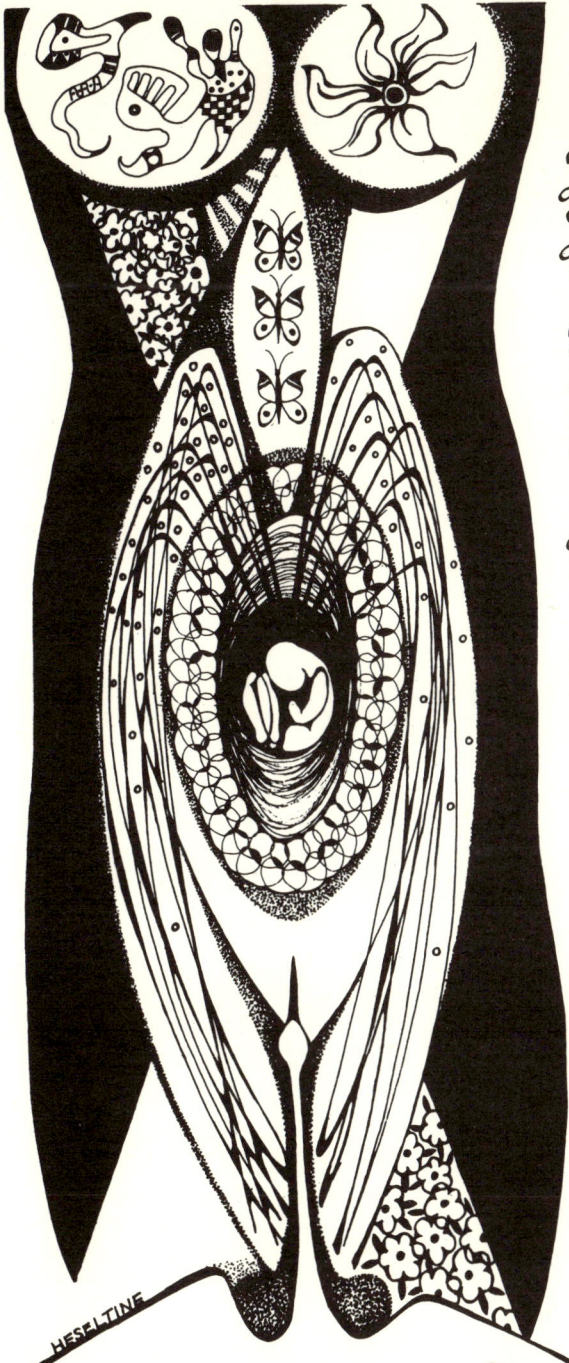

For an unborn child

May there be gold
And dumplings,
Horizons
Amethyst with spinning gazelles
Wheels rimmed in light.

May Great Panjandrum
Pacing bent at the hips, hands in check-trouser pocket,
Coat-tails flapping,
Wink, turn a blind eye
Slipping sixpences.

May two Sandmen,
Also check-trousered,
Brokers' men to the Queen of Faërie,
Sweep oceans of dream through your windows each night.

May the tiniest nameless one
Parachute down from his gannet's wing
With fistfuls of spindrift,
While badger
Shambles up with a mouthful of moly
Checkmating all spells.

May the wise procession of crimson and scarlet
Break into dance at your christening
Till wicked godmothers' blackened gnarls
Blossom like vines jumped from spring into vintage.

Oh may the high season
Catch-as-catch-can with cowslips and hazelnuts
Releasing a million Red Admiral
Troubadours ogling the toadflax.

And may bright water
Shake out his polythene sheets of sunsplash
Spreading a smooth swan's way.
First stop Avalon.

Birth of Aphrodite

Came down the cloud
Paler than amethyst, pale
As the sheen on a robe of cream
Satin tinged by the sunrise.
Came down the cloud,
And the lake burst in a thousand
Splinters of beryl and topaz
Whistling up kingfishers hidden in droplets of dew
Splash fizzle and change
Into dragonfly wings as the light
Splutters and cackles and catches the ripples
In cloak-swirling satin swung by a wind
A kingfisher plunging river
Down gullies of crystal and quartz
Facet on facet on facet of
Diamonds piling the kingfisher pictures
The silver refracted reflections
The forward and backward, backward and forward reflections,
Till there, there, there in the waterdrops
Somewhere, reflected? — refracted? —
Somewhere — there — where — no — the face of the goddess,
Lips eyes, smiles eyes kisses,
Somewhere, scattered through diamonds of water
Held in deep leaves, in lakes of emerald
Where tall green ladies receive her . . .

Neat men will crack as she winds them tighter,
Tighter, tighter, with creaking of winches,
Straps them stiff to a pine and then leaves them,
Screaming, alone with the soughing of branches . . .

Fog rising . . .

Staring of wolves . . .

Cucumber girl
Sliver of water under the moon
Slicing the melon and stepping aside
Hurl those oranges after the sun.

Vanishing rind
Chasing the granite out of the bay
Slip on the stones and sugar the tide
And hurl those oranges after the sun.

The pearl-plunge

      Others have grabbed the gold, girl,
      You've got a basketful.
      Castles of panther 'n antelope,
          candyfloss over the sand,
               nutcracker stepladder sackfuls of tumbling September
      You'll get the pearl, girl.
      Red-legged whistling on waves-a-breaking
          oyster-catch in with the tide girl
      You'll get the pearl.
      Candle in cloister, swing on the chandelier
          knocking the bongoes for elephants hiding inside
              and in with the tide girl
      Diving through green volcanoes of foliage
      Gliding down angelfish palace of icicles,
      Panther and castle, candle and candyfloss
      In with the tide and pearl girl,
      Into the plunge for the pearl now.

Full-fed

Each evening we bounded
Leopard and antelope over the sand
And crashed to the kill.

Then like Valhalla's boars
Returned to be killed once more

And after each kill the lion lay down with the lamb.

There was plenty of feast to feed the cock-crow
Full of morning and mockery.

The farm grew fat, happy at our hunting.

When we have fallen
There will still be our bones for the picking.

Green moon

Green moon you'll howl with envy
And the lizard witch'll scream.
Poking up through the clinkers
A black tulip bulges
Spurting his starlight
Through oceans of heaving marjoram
Fastens our thirsty limbs
To the stoop of a falcon's wings.

The doom-breakers

—for your sole sake
Heaven has put away the stroke of her doom,
So great her portion in that peace you make
By merely walking in a room.
                    —W.B. Yeats

They do appear . .
Walking in tenderness, dew about them,
Footprints that catapult primroses.
Snapping the stalks of justice, immoral as saints.
Never on the way to anywhere in particular.
Strolling through space, occasionally coinciding
With earth's well-timed 1000 MPH revolutions.
They do appear — you lie denying it —
Swinging from the rings of justice like gibbons,
Till Heaven's brutal pendulum shakes with laughter
Forgetting its metronome mark . . .
                    for a catch of breath.

Manstain

Down paths of green horses
Pale fishes of light
Mouthing the seaweed of oak trees
He came
Man
Chlorine-faced, moonwalking backwards
Fish blowing out of his eyes.
The forest blazed with a fire of children
Red plastic and silver paper
Children danced bubbles of innocence.
All horses died.
Fish choked, their silver scales
Bleached dull, to a phosphorus glaze.
The man
Fought his fire with shouts of semen:
"I am your green horse, your pale fishes,
I am your path, it is I that make forest."
All his seed was shouting children
Red plastic silver paper children
Red bubbles of innocence gobbling the earth.

The bee's song to the dead-nettle

Acrobat taste
Head over heels in a splutter of petals
Free-falling nine leagues with white streamers
Glistening the hair of my somersault into the sun,
Trumpet, white trumpet of nectar,
Spinning the world till it shreds into breezes of sugar,
Here at the still
Centre
Scented
I
Drunk
Sleep.

Shula

Out of the sea Shula
Black in the moonlight
Come with your house-cracking back-breaking fingers
To flatten the sleep
of the weetabix-eaters.
Slide from the deep
Octopus holes with your eyes phosphorescent
Spinning your tidal web
Round the corpse of this village of lovers
While giant snails
Trail slime from your sea to the smooth
Black marks where the cottages were.
Shula, unfasten your hair . . .

Ravish us . . .

Carbon-monoxide

Octopus carbon-monoxide smearing the land asleep.
Over the sheep-dazzled green
Smoothing its blanket of grease-dropping grey
Blight-staining the grass as it wipes
The sheep flesh vapourised
To mould-black skeletons.
Chuckling poison squats on the withering ground.
Like Ganges Indians we bathe our faces, our tongues
In the sweet chocolate excrement,
The coal-tar coloured and flavoured
Goo of pure progress rationalising our land.

Vesuvius treacle.

Afterwards nothing.

Gargoyle

I've bin finkin'. If I was God,
I'd lay off the colour green.
I'd have mauve peas in orange pods,
Paint the grass ultramarine
And the leaves all shocking pink.
God could be more like Antonioni
Who goes round painting his beetroot grey.
But He oughter get weaving the opposite way
And stroll round painting his trees vermilion
Instead of those dingy browns
That make parrots look so phoney.
God, I grant you, may be brilliant
At nuclear physics, but he's one of the clowns
When it comes to mixing a palette.
He oughter pop down to my seaside chalet.
I'm preparing spray guns in psychedelic patterns —
Magenta, luminous lemon, cerise —
For squirting at sparrers, stray dogs, tabby kittens,
And touching up God's dreary old trees.
If I'd a' been given the job of Divine Creation
I'd a' made that Garden of Eden look as bright as a petrol station.

Translations from the Greek

Three songs from 'THE BIRDS' by Aristophanes

The Hoopoe's Aubade

    Open your eyes, my love.
    Open your eyes.
    Remember the tune that seemed to rise
    Out of your lips when our child died,
    Remember the holy tune.
    Brown throat
    Vibrate
    The holy tune
    Till amplified
    Through bindweed trumpets it reaches right
    Up where by Zeus' throne
    Phoebus Apollo with golden hair
    Twangs on his harp till all the immortals there
    Are singing and dancing and shouting with delight.

The Hoopoe's Invocation of the Birds

    Yipipee yipipee, yipipee yipipee.
    Hither come hither come hither come hither.
    Yeepipipy yeepipipy, yeepipipy yee.
    Here to me everyone dressed in feathers.
    Yeepipipy yeepipipy yee.
    You who live in the well-sown fields
    Eating the barley and eating the seeds,
    Come in your thousands, chirp your sweet song.
    Tyo tyo tyo, tyo tyo tyo. Tyo tyo tyo, tyo tyo tyo.

    You who follow the farmer's harrow
    Twittering round the fresh-ploughed furrows,
    Come in your thousands, cheep your sweet song,
    Tyo tyo tyo, tyo tyo tyo. Tyo tyo, tyo tyo tyo.

You who are building in apple trees
And have hidden your nests in the ivy leaves,
Raspberry red-currant eaters stop for a moment
      and fly to me here.
Treoto treoto, tototo breex.

You who snap up the humming gnats
Where the fens stretch fertile and flat
Fork-tail blue-back red-throat white-bellied
      swallow swoop to me here.
Divers and gannets draw near,
Leave the sea, birds with long necks are gathering.
All of you, fly to me here.

The Nightingale Song

    Spirit with speckled breast
    Come follow me
    Through thickets, up scree,
    To a nest
    In a cluster of rowan berries,
    Where my brown throat
    Shall sing what you taught me.
    There I shall dance to the nymphs' down-derries
    Where Phrynichus once like a bee
    Knelt sucking nectar out of your melodies.

    So shall the swans cry
    To the River-king
    With clamouring wings
    And fly
    Low over endless marshes.
    The sound in a wave
    Flows up to heaven,
    Winds cease for the cattle to listen
    And the hounds' fur stands on end
    While spirits stumble in breathless astonishment.

from the Parabasis of 'THE BIRDS"

    Humans, you live in the shadow, you live like leaves.
    You incompetent creatures of dust, and feeble as frail,
    Tossed without wings to death like a dream in a gale,
    Listen to how our timeless order lives.
    Listen to us who have infinite space in our thoughts.
    Only from us will you hear truth properly taught.
    We'll tell you the facts in the story of evolution
    Till even Prodicus asks for absolution.

    In the beginning darkness covers the deep.
    No earth, no air, no heaven. But over Hell's sludge and slag
    Night folds her ebony wings, sits down and lays an egg.
    Out of the egg, at the moment when winter goes to sleep
    Sprang love, with wings on his back like a golden storm.
    He leapt into bed with Chaos and out of that marriage
    Our race was hatched. Into the light we hurried
    Up where there had been nothing till Love fell into her arms.
    Nothing was married to Nothing, then heaven and sea,
    Earth and the blessed gods and heroes were born.
    So we are the oldest spirits, we are the dawn,
    We are the flying founders of Love's fraternity.

The meeting of Odysseus and Penelope

from the 'ODYSSEY', book 23 (lines 25-38; 85-116; 153-241)

For twenty years Odysseus has been away. Penelope has remained true to his memory while a crowd of rich and idle young men have feasted in her hall and pestered her to remarry. At last, however, Odysseus has come home, disguised as an old beggar. He has killed all the suitors, and been recognised by the old nurse Eurycleia.

* * *

But her kind old nurse • Eurycleia answered:
"It's true I'm telling you. • No tricks, dear girl.
Your husband Odysseus • is home, he's here.
He's the stranger • who was sneered at by everyone.
For some time • Telemachus knew.
But he's a close one. • Kept quiet, he did;
Till they could pay back • those proud layabouts."
Penelope excitedly • sprang out of bed,
Tears streaming down, • seized the old woman,
Words coming • in cascades on top of each other:
"Do tell me nurse, • dear nurse, do tell me,
Has he really, truly, • arrived? Is he here?
How could he lay into • those louts on his own?
How could he, if they all • kept together inside?"

Then down from her room, • running, her mind
A confusion: — Shall I stand • far away from him
Asking him questions, • or embrace him immediately,
Taking his hands • and head and kissing them?
But once she's stepped over • the stone threshold
She went and sat opposite • Odysseus in the firelight
By the far wall. • He was waiting for her
Sitting against a pillar, • expecting his brave wife
To say something • as soon as she saw him.
But she sat there, • struck dumb with shock.
At one moment • meeting his gaze,
At another not recognising him, • for the rags hanging round him.
Telemachus called out • coldly, saying:
"Mother, you're an unmother. • What a mentality. Frigid.
Why sit so far away • from father? Why don't you
Sit by him and ask him • about everything?
No other woman • would be so stubborn
As to hold off from her man, • when he's home at last
After twenty years • and tired out.
Your heart's strong all right. • Strong as stone."
Out of her prudence • Penelope answered:
"Son, my mind's • stupefied inside me.
I can't form the words, • let alone phrase questions,
Can't even meet • his eyes, but if it's really
Odysseus, my husband, • home, we'll know.
We've got secrets • concealed from everyone."
Odysseus smiled. He'd endured a lot.
Quickly he spoke • to his son Telemachus:
"Telemachus, leave • the lady to question me
Here in the hall. • She'll understand soon.
Because I'm foul, • with filthy clothes on,
She can't admit to herself • me to be me."

So Odysseus sensibly • ordered a bath
From housekeeper Eurynome, • and olive oil.
Bathed and anointed, • with a new tunic,
A fine robe and • flowing from his head
A glory poured over him • by the goddess Athene,
He appeared taller; • thickset; from his head
Hair hanging in curls • like hyacinth flowers.
As when a smith gilds • silver with gold —
A skilled craftsman • from the school of Hephaestus
And Pallas Athene • with pieces of all sorts to his credit —
So Odysseus was gilded • with grace of body,
Seemed like a god • stepping out of the bathtub.
Back to the hall now, • the high seat he'd left.
Sat down facing his wife, • and said to her:
"Lady, the gods • did give you a strong heart,
The stubbornest will • of all women in the world.
What other woman • would have the nerve
To hold off from her man • when he's home at last
After twenty years, • and tired out.
Make me a bed • by myself, nurse.
On my own. She's turned • into iron, my wife."
Then Penelope • prudently answered:
"Sir, I'm not proud; • or scornful. I'm far
Too amazed. But I do • remember the husband
Who left Ithaca • in a long-oared ship.
Still . . .
        Eurycleia • spread blankets,
Sheepskins and rugs, • shining and clean,
Plenty of them, • and pull his bed
Out of the bedroom, • the one he built himself."
This was her husband's • test. Odysseus
Angrily answered • his over-careful wife:
"Lady, that's a terrible • thing to have said.
Who's moved my bed? • That'd be mighty hard,
However clever he was, • unless there came a god
Who'd easily transport it • to another country.
But no man, however strong, • could shift it easily,
Wedge crowbar into • that wonder of a bed.
I made it myself; — • Remember? — no-one else.

Inside our enclosure • that olive tree,
Bushy, plenty of leaves, • in its prime and flourishing.
Trunk perfect as a • pillar. Round it
I built our bedroom, • brought that off.
Close fitting rocks, • and a roof over,
Fixed tight-fitting • well-fastened doors.
Next lopped the branches • from that leafy olive
Rough-hacked the trunk • from the root upwards,
Smoothed it with the adze • — mighty skilled job —
Straightened it with my line. • Shaped the bed-post,
Bored the holes • one by one with my gimlet.
I began with the post. • Now, the bed complete,
Right to the end, • I inlaid it with gold,
Silver, ivory • and stretched across it
Red straps • of shining ox-hide.
That's our secret. Is it there still?
Is it still there, • or has someone moved it?
Chopped down the trunk, • and taken it away?"
Then her knees buckled, • her brave front collapsed.
This was their secret. • It was certainly Odysseus.
Weeping she runs at him, • round his neck
Flinging her arms, • His face kissed all over.
"Odysseus, Odysseus. • Don't be angry, you're always
Wiser than everyone. • Oh we've had our troubles.
Gods with a grudge • against us, in case
We'd stay by each other's • side, delight
In each other's youth, • and then into old age
Saunter together.
Don't blame me dear, • don't be angry
'Cause I didn't embrace you • the instant I saw you.
Inside me there's always • the shuddering thought
Of someone tricking me • by his talk. Oh there are,
There are plenty of men • who plan tricks like that.
But now . . now clearly • you know our secret,
Our bed secret. • No one else knows.
You and me only, • and our old nurse
That father sent with me • on our wedding day
To watch the door • of our wedding chamber.
I am persuaded, • stubborn that I am."

At her words a great weeping • welled up in him.
Holding his wife • he wept, his brave,
His dear, courageous, • careful wife.
Like land-gladness, • looming over swimmers,
Their well-made ship • smashed by Poseidon,
Wind and swollen • waves piled on to it,
Few from the grey sea • grappling shorewards,
Curdles of salt • crusting their flesh;
Gladly the land • they grip, escaping disaster.
So to her was her husband a gladness.
Her white arms from his neck • would never leave go.
And they couldn't stop crying.

Orestes' urn

from Sophocles' 'ELECTRA' (lines 1126-1170)

Electra's father, Agamemnon, has been killed by Clytemnestra his wife and her lover Aegisthus. All that Electra has to live for is the hope that one day her brother Orestes will return and avenge their father's death. Now she has been given an urn full of ashes and told that these are the ashes of Orestes.

Clutching the urn she speaks.

ELECTRA:

>This was the man that of all the world
>I loved the most. And here's the scraps,
>What's left of Orestes. Look how I welcome you,
>Look at my greeting — different from when
>I waved you goodbye. I pick you up
>In my hands, a nothing. Oh I sent away
>All the brightness out of our home boy.
>Oh if only you'd passed away before,
>Before I let you slip through my fingers
>On to foreign earth, protecting you
>From the murderers here. But on that day
>At that moment you should have died
>And received your place in our father's burial.
>Now it's away from home, it's a foreign country,
>It's a mean death, it's away from your sister.
>Not with my hands to love you, to hold you,
>To adorn you with water, raise from the ashes
>Your sad small corpse in the proper ritual.
>Hands of strangers attended you boy.
>Miserable weight in a miserable pot.
>No.
>Oh how I cradled you once upon a time
>Uselessly, uselessly . . .
>Oh how lovely it was to look after you.

I was the mother who loved you — not her.
I was your servants, I was your nurse.
I was the sister you always called for.
All gone, in one day.
You're dead. You've snatched it all.
Like a storm, gone. Father's dead.
I'm dying with you; you're gone, you're dead.
Enemies laughing. Mad with joy
Our mother unmother — and so often you promised
In your secret letters that you'd come back
And break her. Oh you and me
We've got an unlucky spirit that crushed you.
Look how you arrived to meet me
Not in your lithe young body, but ashes.
Dust, a shadow. Useless — oh no —
No . . .
What a stupid shape. No. No.
What an awful thing. Oh no . . .
I sent you away, and you've killed me boy.
You've killed me, my dear brother.
So come on, let me in to your little hut,
Your little nothingness, I'm your nothing sister.
I'm coming to live with you for ever.
When you were here we shared everything.
So now don't stop me from sharing your grave.
For the dead, I don't see them suffering pain.

The death of Oedipus

from Sophocles' 'OEDIPUS AT COLONUS' (lines 1566-1578)

Oedipus has at last come to the end of his wandering. He leaves the stage, walking to a mysterious death that no one is allowed to watch except King Theseus, while the chorus of old men chant a prayer for his passing.

CHORUS

>Dare it be right for me, goddess unnameable
>Dare it be right t'adore thee
>Lord of the drowned in night
>Aidoneus Underworld.
>Take all pain from his passing
>Pain of the horror screaming.
>Let him gently achieve
>The way where all must disappear
>In the river of Hell and the valley of bones.
>Look, look, the marked face, the crass
>Permeation of his pain.
>Is there a power, below, to aid him.
>
>Goddess and queen of dark where the untameable
>Beast of your secret threshold
>Trodden by all mankind
>Must sleep, sleep, sleep, growl, growl
>Through deep caves, never muzzled
>Sentry for everlasting
>As the stories have told.
>Oh Lord, earth's child and child of Hell,
>Oh Lord I pray that a peace may fall,
>Lord guide this man through the waste
>Through the black expanse of bones.
>On Thee I call Lord, the sleep unending.